Want free goodies?
Email us at planner@pbleu.com

 @PapeterieBleu

 @Papeterie Bleu

Shop our other books at
www.pbleu.com

Wholesale distribution through Ingram Content Group
www.ingramcontent.com/publishers/distribution/wholesale

For questions and customer service, email us at
support@pbleu.com

JANUARY 2019

S	M	T	W	T	F	S
		1	2	3	4	5
6	7	8	9	10	11	12
13	14	15	16	17	18	19
20	21	22	23	24	25	26
27	28	29	30	31		

FEBRUARY 2019

S	M	T	W	T	F	S
					1	2
3	4	5	6	7	8	9
10	11	12	13	14	15	16
17	18	19	20	21	22	23
24	25	26	27	28		

MARCH 2019

S	M	T	W	T	F	S
					1	2
3	4	5	6	7	8	9
10	11	12	13	14	15	16
17	18	19	20	21	22	23
24	25	26	27	28	29	30
31						

APRIL 2019

S	M	T	W	T	F	S
	1	2	3	4	5	6
7	8	9	10	11	12	13
14	15	16	17	18	19	20
21	22	23	24	25	26	27
28	29	30				

MAY 2019

S	M	T	W	T	F	S
			1	2	3	4
5	6	7	8	9	10	11
12	13	14	15	16	17	18
19	20	21	22	23	24	25
26	27	28	29	30	31	

JUNE 2019

S	M	T	W	T	F	S
						1
2	3	4	5	6	7	8
9	10	11	12	13	14	15
16	17	18	19	20	21	22
23	24	25	26	27	28	29
30						

JULY 2019

S	M	T	W	T	F	S
	1	2	3	4	5	6
7	8	9	10	11	12	13
14	15	16	17	18	19	20
21	22	23	24	25	26	27
28	29	30	31			

AUGUST 2019

S	M	T	W	T	F	S
				1	2	3
4	5	6	7	8	9	10
11	12	13	14	15	16	17
18	19	20	21	22	23	24
25	26	27	28	29	30	31

SEPTEMBER 2019

S	M	T	W	T	F	S
1	2	3	4	5	6	7
8	9	10	11	12	13	14
15	16	17	18	19	20	21
22	23	24	25	26	27	28
29	30					

OCTOBER 2019

S	M	T	W	T	F	S
		1	2	3	4	5
6	7	8	9	10	11	12
13	14	15	16	17	18	19
20	21	22	23	24	25	26
27	28	29	30	31		

NOVEMBER 2019

S	M	T	W	T	F	S
					1	2
3	4	5	6	7	8	9
10	11	12	13	14	15	16
17	18	19	20	21	22	23
24	25	26	27	28	29	30

DECEMBER 2019

S	M	T	W	T	F	S
1	2	3	4	5	6	7
8	9	10	11	12	13	14
15	16	17	18	19	20	21
22	23	24	25	26	27	28
29	30	31				

2020 YEARLY REVIEW

JANUARY 2020

S	M	T	W	T	F	S
			1	2	3	4
5	6	7	8	9	10	11
12	13	14	15	16	17	18
19	20	21	22	23	24	25
26	27	28	29	30	31	

FEBRUARY 2020

S	M	T	W	T	F	S
						1
2	3	4	5	6	7	8
9	10	11	12	13	14	15
16	17	18	19	20	21	22
23	24	25	26	27	28	29

MARCH 2020

S	M	T	W	T	F	S
1	2	3	4	5	6	7
8	9	10	11	12	13	14
15	16	17	18	19	20	21
22	23	24	25	26	27	28
29	30	31				

APRIL 2020

S	M	T	W	T	F	S
			1	2	3	4
5	6	7	8	9	10	11
12	13	14	15	16	17	18
19	20	21	22	23	24	25
26	27	28	29	30		

MAY 2020

S	M	T	W	T	F	S
					1	2
3	4	5	6	7	8	9
10	11	12	13	14	15	16
17	18	19	20	21	22	23
24	25	26	27	28	29	30
31						

JUNE 2020

S	M	T	W	T	F	S
	1	2	3	4	5	6
7	8	9	10	11	12	13
14	15	16	17	18	19	20
21	22	23	24	25	26	27
28	29	30				

JULY 2020

S	M	T	W	T	F	S
			1	2	3	4
5	6	7	8	9	10	11
12	13	14	15	16	17	18
19	20	21	22	23	24	25
26	27	28	29	30	31	

AUGUST 2020

S	M	T	W	T	F	S
						1
2	3	4	5	6	7	8
9	10	11	12	13	14	15
16	17	18	19	20	21	22
23	24	25	26	27	28	29
30	31					

SEPTEMBER 2020

S	M	T	W	T	F	S
		1	2	3	4	5
6	7	8	9	10	11	12
13	14	15	16	17	18	19
20	21	22	23	24	25	26
27	28	29	30			

OCTOBER 2020

S	M	T	W	T	F	S
				1	2	3
4	5	6	7	8	9	10
11	12	13	14	15	16	17
18	19	20	21	22	23	24
25	26	27	28	29	30	31

NOVEMBER 2020

S	M	T	W	T	F	S
1	2	3	4	5	6	7
8	9	10	11	12	13	14
15	16	17	18	19	20	21
22	23	24	25	26	27	28
29	30					

DECEMBER 2020

S	M	T	W	T	F	S
		1	2	3	4	5
6	7	8	9	10	11	12
13	14	15	16	17	18	19
20	21	22	23	24	25	26
27	28	29	30	31		

JANUARY 2021

S	M	T	W	T	F	S
					1	2
3	4	5	6	7	8	9
10	11	12	13	14	15	16
17	18	19	20	21	22	23
24	25	26	27	28	29	30
31						

FEBRUARY 2021

S	M	T	W	T	F	S
	1	2	3	4	5	6
7	8	9	10	11	12	13
14	15	16	17	18	19	20
21	22	23	24	25	26	27
28						

MARCH 2021

S	M	T	W	T	F	S
	1	2	3	4	5	6
7	8	9	10	11	12	13
14	15	16	17	18	19	20
21	22	23	24	25	26	27
28	29	30	31			

APRIL 2021

S	M	T	W	T	F	S
				1	2	3
4	5	6	7	8	9	10
11	12	13	14	15	16	17
18	19	20	21	22	23	24
25	26	27	28	29	30	

MAY 2021

S	M	T	W	T	F	S
						1
2	3	4	5	6	7	8
9	10	11	12	13	14	15
16	17	18	19	20	21	22
23	24	25	26	27	28	29
30	31					

JUNE 2021

S	M	T	W	T	F	S
		1	2	3	4	5
6	7	8	9	10	11	12
13	14	15	16	17	18	19
20	21	22	23	24	25	26
27	28	29	30			

JULY 2021

S	M	T	W	T	F	S
				1	2	3
4	5	6	7	8	9	10
11	12	13	14	15	16	17
18	19	20	21	22	23	24
25	26	27	28	29	30	31

AUGUST 2021

S	M	T	W	T	F	S
1	2	3	4	5	6	7
8	9	10	11	12	13	14
15	16	17	18	19	20	21
22	23	24	25	26	27	28
29	30	31				

SEPTEMBER 2021

S	M	T	W	T	F	S
			1	2	3	4
5	6	7	8	9	10	11
12	13	14	15	16	17	18
19	20	21	22	23	24	25
26	27	28	29	30		

OCTOBER 2021

S	M	T	W	T	F	S
					1	2
3	4	5	6	7	8	9
10	11	12	13	14	15	16
17	18	19	20	21	22	23
24	25	26	27	28	29	30
31						

NOVEMBER 2021

S	M	T	W	T	F	S
	1	2	3	4	5	6
7	8	9	10	11	12	13
14	15	16	17	18	19	20
21	22	23	24	25	26	27
28	29	30				

DECEMBER 2021

S	M	T	W	T	F	S
			1	2	3	4
5	6	7	8	9	10	11
12	13	14	15	16	17	18
19	20	21	22	23	24	25
26	27	28	29	30	31	

JULY

SUNDAY	MONDAY	TUESDAY	WEDNESDAY
	1	2	3
7	8	9	10
14	15	16	17
21	22	23	24
28	29	30	31

2019

THURSDAY	FRIDAY	SATURDAY	NOTES
4	5	6	☐ ___
11	12	13	☐ ___
18	19	20	☐ ___
25	26	27	☐ ___

JUNE

S	M	T	W	T	F	S
						1
2	3	4	5	6	7	8
9	10	11	12	13	14	15
16	17	18	19	20	21	22
23	24	25	26	27	28	29
30						

JULY

S	M	T	W	T	F	S
	1	2	3	4	5	6
7	8	9	10	11	12	13
14	15	16	17	18	19	20
21	22	23	24	25	26	27
28	29	30	31			

1
MONODAY

- [ ]
- [ ]
- [ ]
- [ ]
- [ ]
- [ ]
- [ ]
- [ ]

2
TUESDAY

- [ ]
- [ ]
- [ ]
- [ ]
- [ ]
- [ ]
- [ ]
- [ ]

3
WEDNESDAY

- [ ]
- [ ]
- [ ]
- [ ]
- [ ]
- [ ]
- [ ]
- [ ]

4
THURSDAY

- [ ]
- [ ]
- [ ]
- [ ]
- [ ]
- [ ]
- [ ]
- [ ]

Wherever you are, be all there.

– Jim Elliot

JULY '19

5
FRIDAY

- [ ] _____
- [ ] _____
- [ ] _____
- [ ] _____
- [ ] _____
- [ ] _____
- [ ] _____
- [ ] _____

6
SATURDAY

- [ ] _____
- [ ] _____
- [ ] _____
- [ ] _____
- [ ] _____
- [ ] _____
- [ ] _____
- [ ] _____

7
SUNDAY

- [ ] _____
- [ ] _____
- [ ] _____
- [ ] _____
- [ ] _____
- [ ] _____
- [ ] _____
- [ ] _____

8
MONADY

☐
☐
☐
☐
☐
☐
☐
☐

9
TUESDAY

☐
☐
☐
☐
☐
☐
☐
☐

10
WEDNESDAY

☐
☐
☐
☐
☐
☐
☐
☐

11
THURSDAY

☐
☐
☐
☐
☐
☐
☐
☐

Kindness is the noblest weapon to conquer with.
– Thomas Fuller

JULY

12
FRIDAY

- ☐ _____
- ☐ _____
- ☐ _____
- ☐ _____
- ☐ _____
- ☐ _____
- ☐ _____
- ☐ _____

13
SATURDAY

- ☐ _____
- ☐ _____
- ☐ _____
- ☐ _____
- ☐ _____
- ☐ _____
- ☐ _____
- ☐ _____

14
SUNDAY

- ☐ _____
- ☐ _____
- ☐ _____
- ☐ _____
- ☐ _____
- ☐ _____
- ☐ _____
- ☐ _____

15
MONDAY

☐
☐
☐
☐
☐
☐
☐
☐

16
TUESDAY

☐
☐
☐
☐
☐
☐
☐
☐

17
WEDNESDAY

☐
☐
☐
☐
☐
☐
☐
☐

18
THURSDAY

☐
☐
☐
☐
☐
☐
☐
☐

I have learned that to be with those I love is enough.

– Walt Whitman

JULY

19
FRIDAY

- ☐ _____
- ☐ _____
- ☐ _____
- ☐ _____
- ☐ _____
- ☐ _____
- ☐ _____
- ☐ _____

20
SATURDAY

- ☐ _____
- ☐ _____
- ☐ _____
- ☐ _____
- ☐ _____
- ☐ _____
- ☐ _____
- ☐ _____

21
SUNDAY

- ☐ _____
- ☐ _____
- ☐ _____
- ☐ _____
- ☐ _____
- ☐ _____
- ☐ _____
- ☐ _____

22
MONDAY

- [ ]
- [ ]
- [ ]
- [ ]
- [ ]
- [ ]
- [ ]
- [ ]

23
TUESDAY

- [ ]
- [ ]
- [ ]
- [ ]
- [ ]
- [ ]
- [ ]
- [ ]

24
WEDNESDAY

- [ ]
- [ ]
- [ ]
- [ ]
- [ ]
- [ ]
- [ ]
- [ ]

25
THURSDAY

- [ ]
- [ ]
- [ ]
- [ ]
- [ ]
- [ ]
- [ ]
- [ ]

JULY

26
FRIDAY

- [ ] _____
- [ ] _____
- [ ] _____
- [ ] _____
- [ ] _____
- [ ] _____
- [ ] _____
- [ ] _____

27
SATURDAY

- [ ] _____
- [ ] _____
- [ ] _____
- [ ] _____
- [ ] _____
- [ ] _____
- [ ] _____
- [ ] _____

28
SUNDAY

- [ ] _____
- [ ] _____
- [ ] _____
- [ ] _____
- [ ] _____
- [ ] _____
- [ ] _____
- [ ] _____

AUGUST

SUNDAY	MONDAY	TUESDAY	WEDNESDAY
4	5	6	7
11	12	13	14
18	19	20	21
25	26	27	28

2019

THURSDAY	FRIDAY	SATURDAY	NOTES
1	2	3	
8	9	10	
15	16	17	
22	23	24	
29	30	31	

JULY

S	M	T	W	T	F	S
	1	2	3	4	5	6
7	8	9	10	11	12	13
14	15	16	17	18	19	20
21	22	23	24	25	26	27
28	29	30	31			

AUGUST

S	M	T	W	T	F	S
				1	2	3
4	5	6	7	8	9	10
11	12	13	14	15	16	17
18	19	20	21	22	23	24
25	26	27	28	29	30	31

29
MONADY

- [ ]
- [ ]
- [ ]
- [ ]
- [ ]
- [ ]
- [ ]
- [ ]

30
TUESDAY

- [ ]
- [ ]
- [ ]
- [ ]
- [ ]
- [ ]
- [ ]
- [ ]

31
WEDNESDAY

- [ ]
- [ ]
- [ ]
- [ ]
- [ ]
- [ ]
- [ ]
- [ ]

1
THURSDAY

- [ ]
- [ ]
- [ ]
- [ ]
- [ ]
- [ ]
- [ ]
- [ ]

The best preparation for tomorrow is doing your best today.
– H. Jackson Brown, Jr.

JULY-AUG

2
FRIDAY

- [ ]
- [ ]
- [ ]
- [ ]
- [ ]
- [ ]
- [ ]
- [ ]

3
SATURDAY

- [ ]
- [ ]
- [ ]
- [ ]
- [ ]
- [ ]
- [ ]
- [ ]

4
SUNDAY

- [ ]
- [ ]
- [ ]
- [ ]
- [ ]
- [ ]
- [ ]
- [ ]

5
MONODAY

☐
☐
☐
☐
☐
☐
☐
☐

6
TUESDAY

☐
☐
☐
☐
☐
☐
☐
☐

7
WEDNESDAY

☐
☐
☐
☐
☐
☐
☐
☐

8
THURSDAY

☐
☐
☐
☐
☐
☐
☐
☐

Nothing is impossible, the word itself says 'I'm possible'!

– Audrey Hepburn

AUGUST

9
FRIDAY

☐ _____
☐ _____
☐ _____
☐ _____
☐ _____
☐ _____
☐ _____
☐ _____

10
SATURDAY

☐ _____
☐ _____
☐ _____
☐ _____
☐ _____
☐ _____
☐ _____
☐ _____

11
SUNDAY

☐ _____
☐ _____
☐ _____
☐ _____
☐ _____
☐ _____
☐ _____
☐ _____

12
MONDAY

☐
☐
☐
☐
☐
☐
☐
☐

13
TUESDAY

☐
☐
☐
☐
☐
☐
☐
☐

14
WEDNESDAY

☐
☐
☐
☐
☐
☐
☐
☐

15
THURSDAY

☐
☐
☐
☐
☐
☐
☐
☐

Believe you can and you're halfway there.
– Theodore Roosevelt

16
FRIDAY

- ☐ _____
- ☐ _____
- ☐ _____
- ☐ _____
- ☐ _____
- ☐ _____
- ☐ _____
- ☐ _____

17
SATURDAY

- ☐ _____
- ☐ _____
- ☐ _____
- ☐ _____
- ☐ _____
- ☐ _____
- ☐ _____
- ☐ _____

18
SUNDAY

- ☐ _____
- ☐ _____
- ☐ _____
- ☐ _____
- ☐ _____
- ☐ _____
- ☐ _____
- ☐ _____

19
MONDAY

☐
☐
☐
☐
☐
☐
☐
☐

20
TUESDAY

☐
☐
☐
☐
☐
☐
☐
☐

21
WEDNESDAY

☐
☐
☐
☐
☐
☐
☐
☐

22
THURSDAY

☐
☐
☐
☐
☐
☐
☐
☐

Try to be a rainbow in someone's cloud.
– Maya Angelou

AUGUST

23
FRIDAY

☐ _____
☐ _____
☐ _____
☐ _____
☐ _____
☐ _____
☐ _____
☐ _____

24
SATURDAY

☐ _____
☐ _____
☐ _____
☐ _____
☐ _____
☐ _____
☐ _____
☐ _____

25
SUNDAY

☐ _____
☐ _____
☐ _____
☐ _____
☐ _____
☐ _____
☐ _____
☐ _____

SEPTEMBER

SUNDAY	MONDAY	TUESDAY	WEDNESDAY
1	2	3	4
8	9	10	11
15	16	17	18
22	23	24	25
29	30		

2019

THURSDAY	FRIDAY	SATURDAY	NOTES
5	6	7	☐ _____
			☐ _____
			☐ _____
			☐ _____
			☐ _____
			☐ _____
12	13	14	☐ _____
			☐ _____
			☐ _____
			☐ _____
			☐ _____
			☐ _____
19	20	21	☐ _____
			☐ _____
			☐ _____
			☐ _____
			☐ _____
			☐ _____
26	27	28	☐ _____

AUGUST

S	M	T	W	T	F	S
				1	2	3
4	5	6	7	8	9	10
11	12	13	14	15	16	17
18	19	20	21	22	23	24
25	26	27	28	29	30	31

SEPTEMBER

S	M	T	W	T	F	S
1	2	3	4	5	6	7
8	9	10	11	12	13	14
15	16	17	18	19	20	21
22	23	24	25	26	27	28
29	30					

26
MONDAY

27
TUESDAY

28
WEDNESDAY

29
THURSDAY

☐
☐
☐
☐
☐
☐
☐
☐

☐
☐
☐
☐
☐
☐
☐
☐

☐
☐
☐
☐
☐
☐
☐
☐

☐
☐
☐
☐
☐
☐
☐
☐

If opportunity doesn't knock, build a door.
— Milton Berle

AUG-SEP

30
FRIDAY

31
SATURDAY

1
SUNDAY

2
MONDAY

☐
☐
☐
☐
☐
☐
☐
☐

3
TUESDAY

☐
☐
☐
☐
☐
☐
☐
☐

4
WEDNESDAY

☐
☐
☐
☐
☐
☐
☐
☐

5
THURSDAY

☐
☐
☐
☐
☐
☐
☐
☐

No act of kindness, no matter how small, is ever wasted.

– Aesop

SEPTEMBER

6
FRIDAY

- ☐
- ☐
- ☐
- ☐
- ☐
- ☐
- ☐
- ☐

7
SATURDAY

- ☐
- ☐
- ☐
- ☐
- ☐
- ☐
- ☐
- ☐

8
SUNDAY

- ☐
- ☐
- ☐
- ☐
- ☐
- ☐
- ☐
- ☐

9
MONDAY

10
TUESDAY

11
WEDNESDAY

12
THURSDAY

SEPTEMBER

13
FRIDAY

14
SATURDAY

15
SUNDAY

16
MONDAY

☐
☐
☐
☐
☐
☐
☐
☐

17
TUESDAY

☐
☐
☐
☐
☐
☐
☐
☐

18
WEDNESDAY

☐
☐
☐
☐
☐
☐
☐
☐

19
THURSDAY

☐
☐
☐
☐
☐
☐
☐
☐

A girl should be two things: classy and fabulous.
— Coco Chanel

SEPTEMBER

20
FRIDAY

- [ ]
- [ ]
- [ ]
- [ ]
- [ ]
- [ ]
- [ ]
- [ ]

21
SATURDAY

- [ ]
- [ ]
- [ ]
- [ ]
- [ ]
- [ ]
- [ ]
- [ ]

22
SUNDAY

- [ ]
- [ ]
- [ ]
- [ ]
- [ ]
- [ ]
- [ ]
- [ ]

23
MONDAY

24
TUESDAY

25
WEDNESDAY

26
THURSDAY

SEPTEMBER

27
FRIDAY

- [ ]
- [ ]
- [ ]
- [ ]
- [ ]
- [ ]
- [ ]
- [ ]

28
SATURDAY

- [ ]
- [ ]
- [ ]
- [ ]
- [ ]
- [ ]
- [ ]
- [ ]

29
SUNDAY

- [ ]
- [ ]
- [ ]
- [ ]
- [ ]
- [ ]
- [ ]
- [ ]

OCTOBER

SUNDAY	MONDAY	TUESDAY	WEDNESDAY
		1	2
6	7	8	9
13	14	15	16
20	21	22	23
27	28	29	30

2019

THURSDAY	FRIDAY	SATURDAY	NOTES
3	4	5	☐ _____ ☐ _____ ☐ _____ ☐ _____ ☐ _____ ☐ _____
10	11	12	☐ _____ ☐ _____ ☐ _____ ☐ _____ ☐ _____ ☐ _____
17	18	19	☐ _____ ☐ _____ ☐ _____ ☐ _____ ☐ _____ ☐ _____
24	25	26	
31			

SEPTEMBER

S	M	T	W	T	F	S
1	2	3	4	5	6	7
8	9	10	11	12	13	14
15	16	17	18	19	20	21
22	23	24	25	26	27	28
29	30					

OCTOBER

S	M	T	W	T	F	S
		1	2	3	4	5
6	7	8	9	10	11	12
13	14	15	16	17	18	19
20	21	22	23	24	25	26
27	28	29	30	31		

30
MONDAY

☐
☐
☐
☐
☐
☐
☐
☐

1
TUESDAY

☐
☐
☐
☐
☐
☐
☐
☐

2
WEDNESDAY

☐
☐
☐
☐
☐
☐
☐
☐

3
THURSDAY

☐
☐
☐
☐
☐
☐
☐
☐

If you can dream it, you can do it.
– Walt Disney

SEP-OCT

4
FRIDAY

☐ _____
☐ _____
☐ _____
☐ _____
☐ _____
☐ _____
☐ _____
☐ _____

5
SATURDAY

☐ _____
☐ _____
☐ _____
☐ _____
☐ _____
☐ _____
☐ _____
☐ _____

6
SUNDAY

☐ _____
☐ _____
☐ _____
☐ _____
☐ _____
☐ _____
☐ _____
☐ _____

7
MONONDAY

☐
☐
☐
☐
☐
☐
☐
☐

8
TUESDAY

☐
☐
☐
☐
☐
☐
☐
☐

9
WEDNESDAY

☐
☐
☐
☐
☐
☐
☐
☐

10
THURSDAY

☐
☐
☐
☐
☐
☐
☐
☐

The secret of getting ahead is getting started.
– Mark Twain

OCTOBER

11
FRIDAY

- [ ]
- [ ]
- [ ]
- [ ]
- [ ]
- [ ]
- [ ]
- [ ]

12
SATURDAY

- [ ]
- [ ]
- [ ]
- [ ]
- [ ]
- [ ]
- [ ]
- [ ]

13
SUNDAY

- [ ]
- [ ]
- [ ]
- [ ]
- [ ]
- [ ]
- [ ]
- [ ]

14
MONDAY

☐
☐
☐
☐
☐
☐
☐
☐

15
TUESDAY

☐
☐
☐
☐
☐
☐
☐
☐

16
WEDNESDAY

☐
☐
☐
☐
☐
☐
☐
☐

17
THURSDAY

☐
☐
☐
☐
☐
☐
☐
☐

Keep your eyes on the stars, and your feet on the ground.
                    – Theodore Roosevelt

OCTOBER

18
FRIDAY

- [ ]
- [ ]
- [ ]
- [ ]
- [ ]
- [ ]
- [ ]
- [ ]

19
SATURDAY

- [ ]
- [ ]
- [ ]
- [ ]
- [ ]
- [ ]
- [ ]
- [ ]

20
SUNDAY

- [ ]
- [ ]
- [ ]
- [ ]
- [ ]
- [ ]
- [ ]
- [ ]

21
MONDAY

22
TUESDAY

23
WEDNESDAY

24
THURSDAY

I have found that if you love life, life will love you
back.
                                            – Arthur Rubinstein

OCTOBER

25
FRIDAY

☐ _____
☐ _____
☐ _____
☐ _____
☐ _____
☐ _____
☐ _____
☐ _____

26
SATURDAY

☐ _____
☐ _____
☐ _____
☐ _____
☐ _____
☐ _____
☐ _____
☐ _____

27
SUNDAY

☐ _____
☐ _____
☐ _____
☐ _____
☐ _____
☐ _____
☐ _____
☐ _____

NOVEMBER

SUNDAY	MONDAY	TUESDAY	WEDNESDAY
3	4	5	6
10	11	12	13
17	18	19	20
24	25	26	27

2019

THURSDAY	FRIDAY	SATURDAY	NOTES
	1	2	☐ _____
			☐ _____
			☐ _____
			☐ _____
			☐ _____
			☐ _____
7	8	9	☐ _____
			☐ _____
			☐ _____
			☐ _____
			☐ _____
			☐ _____
14	15	16	☐ _____
			☐ _____
			☐ _____
			☐ _____
			☐ _____
			☐ _____
21	22	23	
28	29	30	

OCTOBER

S	M	T	W	T	F	S
		1	2	3	4	5
6	7	8	9	10	11	12
13	14	15	16	17	18	19
20	21	22	23	24	25	26
27	28	29	30	31		

NOVEMBER

S	M	T	W	T	F	S
					1	2
3	4	5	6	7	8	9
10	11	12	13	14	15	16
17	18	19	20	21	22	23
24	25	26	27	28	29	30

28
MONDAY

29
TUESDAY

30
WEDNESDAY

31
THURSDAY

☐
☐
☐
☐
☐
☐
☐
☐

☐
☐
☐
☐
☐
☐
☐
☐

☐
☐
☐
☐
☐
☐
☐
☐

☐
☐
☐
☐
☐
☐
☐
☐

There is only one happiness in this life, to love and be loved.

– George Sand

OCT-NOV

1
FRIDAY

2
SATURDAY

3
SUNDAY

4
MONDAY

☐
☐
☐
☐
☐
☐
☐
☐

5
TUESDAY

☐
☐
☐
☐
☐
☐
☐
☐

6
WEDNESDAY

☐
☐
☐
☐
☐
☐
☐
☐

7
THURSDAY

☐
☐
☐
☐
☐
☐
☐
☐

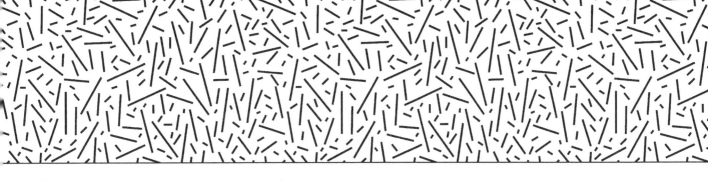

It does not matter how slowly you go as long as you do not stop.

– Confuscious

NOVEMBER

8
FRIDAY

- ☐ _____
- ☐ _____
- ☐ _____
- ☐ _____
- ☐ _____
- ☐ _____
- ☐ _____
- ☐ _____

9
SATURDAY

- ☐ _____
- ☐ _____
- ☐ _____
- ☐ _____
- ☐ _____
- ☐ _____
- ☐ _____
- ☐ _____

10
SUNDAY

- ☐ _____
- ☐ _____
- ☐ _____
- ☐ _____
- ☐ _____
- ☐ _____
- ☐ _____
- ☐ _____

11
MONDAY

- [ ]
- [ ]
- [ ]
- [ ]
- [ ]
- [ ]
- [ ]
- [ ]

12
TUESDAY

- [ ]
- [ ]
- [ ]
- [ ]
- [ ]
- [ ]
- [ ]
- [ ]

13
WEDNESDAY

- [ ]
- [ ]
- [ ]
- [ ]
- [ ]
- [ ]
- [ ]
- [ ]

14
THURSDAY

- [ ]
- [ ]
- [ ]
- [ ]
- [ ]
- [ ]
- [ ]
- [ ]

Accept the challenges so that you can feel the
exhilaration of victory.
                    – George S. Patton

NOVEMBER

15
FRIDAY

- [ ]
- [ ]
- [ ]
- [ ]
- [ ]
- [ ]
- [ ]
- [ ]

16
SATURDAY

- [ ]
- [ ]
- [ ]
- [ ]
- [ ]
- [ ]
- [ ]
- [ ]

17
SUNDAY

- [ ]
- [ ]
- [ ]
- [ ]
- [ ]
- [ ]
- [ ]
- [ ]

18
MONDAY

☐
☐
☐
☐
☐
☐
☐
☐

19
TUESDAY

☐
☐
☐
☐
☐
☐
☐
☐

20
WEDNESDAY

☐
☐
☐
☐
☐
☐
☐
☐

21
THURSDAY

☐
☐
☐
☐
☐
☐
☐
☐

Life isn't about finding yourself. Life is about creating yourself.

– George Bernard Shaw

NOVEMBER

22
FRIDAY

23
SATURDAY

24
SUNDAY

DECEMBER

SUNDAY	MONDAY	TUESDAY	WEDNESDAY
1	2	3	4
8	9	10	11
15	16	17	18
22	23	24	25
29	30	31	

2019

THURSDAY	FRIDAY	SATURDAY	NOTES
5	6	7	
12	13	14	
19	20	21	
26	27	28	

NOVEMBER

S	M	T	W	T	F	S
					1	2
3	4	5	6	7	8	9
10	11	12	13	14	15	16
17	18	19	20	21	22	23
24	25	26	27	28	29	30

DECEMBER

S	M	T	W	T	F	S
1	2	3	4	5	6	7
8	9	10	11	12	13	14
15	16	17	18	19	20	21
22	23	24	25	26	27	28
29	30	31				

25
MONEY

26
TUESDAY

27
WEDNESDAY

28
THURSDAY

In the end, it's not the years in your life that count. It's the life in your years.
– Abraham Lincoln

NOV-DEC

29 FRIDAY

☐ _____
☐ _____
☐ _____
☐ _____
☐ _____
☐ _____
☐ _____
☐ _____

30 SATURDAY

☐ _____
☐ _____
☐ _____
☐ _____
☐ _____
☐ _____
☐ _____
☐ _____

1 SUNDAY

☐ _____
☐ _____
☐ _____
☐ _____
☐ _____
☐ _____
☐ _____
☐ _____

2
MONDAY

☐
☐
☐
☐
☐
☐
☐
☐

3
TUESDAY

☐
☐
☐
☐
☐
☐
☐
☐

4
WEDNESDAY

☐
☐
☐
☐
☐
☐
☐
☐

5
THURSDAY

☐
☐
☐
☐
☐
☐
☐
☐

The purpose of our lives is to be happy.
– Dalai Lama

DECEMBER

6
FRIDAY

- [ ] _____
- [ ] _____
- [ ] _____
- [ ] _____
- [ ] _____
- [ ] _____
- [ ] _____
- [ ] _____

7
SATURDAY

- [ ] _____
- [ ] _____
- [ ] _____
- [ ] _____
- [ ] _____
- [ ] _____
- [ ] _____
- [ ] _____

8
SUNDAY

- [ ] _____
- [ ] _____
- [ ] _____
- [ ] _____
- [ ] _____
- [ ] _____
- [ ] _____
- [ ] _____

9
MONADY

10
TUESDAY

11
WEDNESDAY

12
THURSDAY

DECEMBER

13
FRIDAY

14
SATURDAY

15
SUNDAY

16
MONADY

☐
☐
☐
☐
☐
☐
☐
☐

17
TUESDAY

☐
☐
☐
☐
☐
☐
☐
☐

18
WEDNESDAY

☐
☐
☐
☐
☐
☐
☐
☐

19
THURSDAY

☐
☐
☐
☐
☐
☐
☐
☐

DECEMBER

20
FRIDAY

- [ ] _____
- [ ] _____
- [ ] _____
- [ ] _____
- [ ] _____
- [ ] _____
- [ ] _____
- [ ] _____

21
SATURDAY

- [ ] _____
- [ ] _____
- [ ] _____
- [ ] _____
- [ ] _____
- [ ] _____
- [ ] _____
- [ ] _____

22
SUNDAY

- [ ] _____
- [ ] _____
- [ ] _____
- [ ] _____
- [ ] _____
- [ ] _____
- [ ] _____
- [ ] _____

23
MONDAY

☐
☐
☐
☐
☐
☐
☐
☐

24
TUESDAY

☐
☐
☐
☐
☐
☐
☐
☐

25
WEDNESDAY

☐
☐
☐
☐
☐
☐
☐
☐

26
THURSDAY

☐
☐
☐
☐
☐
☐
☐
☐

The mind is everything. What you think you be-
come.
                                    – Buddha

DECEMBER

27
FRIDAY

- [ ] _____
- [ ] _____
- [ ] _____
- [ ] _____
- [ ] _____
- [ ] _____
- [ ] _____
- [ ] _____

28
SATURDAY

- [ ] _____
- [ ] _____
- [ ] _____
- [ ] _____
- [ ] _____
- [ ] _____
- [ ] _____
- [ ] _____

29
SUNDAY

- [ ] _____
- [ ] _____
- [ ] _____
- [ ] _____
- [ ] _____
- [ ] _____
- [ ] _____
- [ ] _____

JANUARY

SUNDAY	MONDAY	TUESDAY	WEDNESDAY
			1
5	6	7	8
12	13	14	15
19	20	21	22
26	27	28	29

2020

THURSDAY	FRIDAY	SATURDAY	NOTES
2	3	4	☐ _____ ☐ _____ ☐ _____ ☐ _____ ☐ _____ ☐ _____
9	10	11	☐ _____ ☐ _____ ☐ _____ ☐ _____ ☐ _____ ☐ _____
16	17	18	☐ _____ ☐ _____ ☐ _____ ☐ _____ ☐ _____ ☐ _____
23	24	25	
30	31		

JANUARY

S	M	T	W	T	F	S
			1	2	3	4
5	6	7	8	9	10	11
12	13	14	15	16	17	18
19	20	21	22	23	24	25
26	27	28	29	30	31	

FEBRUARY

S	M	T	W	T	F	S
						1
2	3	4	5	6	7	8
9	10	11	12	13	14	15
16	17	18	19	20	21	22
23	24	25	26	27	28	29

30
MONODAY

31
TUESDAY

1
WEDNESDAY

2
THURSDAY

Eighty percent of success is showing up.
– Woody Allen

DEC '19-JAN

3
FRIDAY

- [ ] _____
- [ ] _____
- [ ] _____
- [ ] _____
- [ ] _____
- [ ] _____
- [ ] _____
- [ ] _____

4
SATURDAY

- [ ] _____
- [ ] _____
- [ ] _____
- [ ] _____
- [ ] _____
- [ ] _____
- [ ] _____
- [ ] _____

5
SUNDAY

- [ ] _____
- [ ] _____
- [ ] _____
- [ ] _____
- [ ] _____
- [ ] _____
- [ ] _____
- [ ] _____

6
MONDAY

☐
☐
☐
☐
☐
☐
☐
☐

7
TUESDAY

☐
☐
☐
☐
☐
☐
☐
☐

8
WEDNESDAY

☐
☐
☐
☐
☐
☐
☐
☐

9
THURSDAY

☐
☐
☐
☐
☐
☐
☐
☐

Simplicity is the keynote of all true elegance.
– Coco Chanel

JANUARY

10
FRIDAY

☐ _____
☐ _____
☐ _____
☐ _____
☐ _____
☐ _____
☐ _____
☐ _____

11
SATURDAY

☐ _____
☐ _____
☐ _____
☐ _____
☐ _____
☐ _____
☐ _____
☐ _____

12
SUNDAY

☐ _____
☐ _____
☐ _____
☐ _____
☐ _____
☐ _____
☐ _____
☐ _____

13
MONDAY

14
TUESDAY

15
WEDNESDAY

16
THURSDAY

It always seems impossible until it's done.
– Nelson Mandela

JANUARY

17
FRIDAY

- [ ] _____
- [ ] _____
- [ ] _____
- [ ] _____
- [ ] _____
- [ ] _____
- [ ] _____
- [ ] _____

18
SATURDAY

- [ ] _____
- [ ] _____
- [ ] _____
- [ ] _____
- [ ] _____
- [ ] _____
- [ ] _____
- [ ] _____

19
SUNDAY

- [ ] _____
- [ ] _____
- [ ] _____
- [ ] _____
- [ ] _____
- [ ] _____
- [ ] _____
- [ ] _____

20
MONDAY

☐
☐
☐
☐
☐
☐
☐
☐

21
TUESDAY

☐
☐
☐
☐
☐
☐
☐
☐

22
WEDNESDAY

☐
☐
☐
☐
☐
☐
☐
☐

23
THURSDAY

☐
☐
☐
☐
☐
☐
☐
☐

Live in the sunshine, swim in the sea, drink the
wild air.
                    – Ralph Waldo Emerson

JANUARY

24
FRIDAY

- [ ]
- [ ]
- [ ]
- [ ]
- [ ]
- [ ]
- [ ]
- [ ]

25
SATURDAY

- [ ]
- [ ]
- [ ]
- [ ]
- [ ]
- [ ]
- [ ]
- [ ]

26
SUNDAY

- [ ]
- [ ]
- [ ]
- [ ]
- [ ]
- [ ]
- [ ]
- [ ]

FEBRUARY

SUNDAY	MONDAY	TUESDAY	WEDNESDAY
2	3	4	5
9	10	11	12
16	17	18	19
23	24	25	26

2020

THURSDAY	FRIDAY	SATURDAY	NOTES
		1	☐ _____
			☐ _____
			☐ _____
			☐ _____
			☐ _____
			☐ _____
6	7	8	☐ _____
			☐ _____
			☐ _____
			☐ _____
			☐ _____
			☐ _____
13	14	15	☐ _____
			☐ _____
			☐ _____
			☐ _____
			☐ _____
			☐ _____
20	21	22	
27	28	29	

JANUARY

S	M	T	W	T	F	S
			1	2	3	4
5	6	7	8	9	10	11
12	13	14	15	16	17	18
19	20	21	22	23	24	25
26	27	28	29	30	31	

FEBRUARY

S	M	T	W	T	F	S
						1
2	3	4	5	6	7	8
9	10	11	12	13	14	15
16	17	18	19	20	21	22
23	24	25	26	27	28	29

27
MONDAY

☐
☐
☐
☐
☐
☐
☐
☐

28
TUESDAY

☐
☐
☐
☐
☐
☐
☐
☐

29
WEDNESDAY

☐
☐
☐
☐
☐
☐
☐
☐

30
THURSDAY

☐
☐
☐
☐
☐
☐
☐
☐

> If you ever find yourself in the wrong story, leave.
> – Mo Willems

JAN-FEB

31
FRIDAY

- [ ] _____
- [ ] _____
- [ ] _____
- [ ] _____
- [ ] _____
- [ ] _____
- [ ] _____
- [ ] _____

1
SATURDAY

- [ ] _____
- [ ] _____
- [ ] _____
- [ ] _____
- [ ] _____
- [ ] _____
- [ ] _____
- [ ] _____

2
SUNDAY

- [ ] _____
- [ ] _____
- [ ] _____
- [ ] _____
- [ ] _____
- [ ] _____
- [ ] _____
- [ ] _____

3
MONDAY

4
TUESDAY

5
WEDNESDAY

6
THURSDAY

But all of the magic I have known I've had to
make myself.
                              – Shel Silverstein

FEBRUARY

7
FRIDAY

- [ ] _____
- [ ] _____
- [ ] _____
- [ ] _____
- [ ] _____
- [ ] _____
- [ ] _____
- [ ] _____

8
SATURDAY

- [ ] _____
- [ ] _____
- [ ] _____
- [ ] _____
- [ ] _____
- [ ] _____
- [ ] _____
- [ ] _____

9
SUNDAY

- [ ] _____
- [ ] _____
- [ ] _____
- [ ] _____
- [ ] _____
- [ ] _____
- [ ] _____
- [ ] _____

10
MONADY

_____
_____
_____
_____
_____
_____
_____

11
TUESDAY

_____
_____
_____
_____
_____
_____
_____

12
WEDNESDAY

_____
_____
_____
_____
_____
_____
_____

13
THURSDAY

_____
_____
_____
_____
_____
_____
_____

☐ _____
☐ _____
☐ _____
☐ _____
☐ _____
☐ _____
☐ _____
☐ _____

☐ _____
☐ _____
☐ _____
☐ _____
☐ _____
☐ _____
☐ _____
☐ _____

☐ _____
☐ _____
☐ _____
☐ _____
☐ _____
☐ _____
☐ _____
☐ _____

☐ _____
☐ _____
☐ _____
☐ _____
☐ _____
☐ _____
☐ _____
☐ _____

Be silly. Be honest. Be kind.
– Ralph Waldo Emerson

FEBRUARY

14
FRIDAY

☐ _____
☐ _____
☐ _____
☐ _____
☐ _____
☐ _____
☐ _____
☐ _____

15
SATURDAY

☐ _____
☐ _____
☐ _____
☐ _____
☐ _____
☐ _____
☐ _____
☐ _____

16
SUNDAY

☐ _____
☐ _____
☐ _____
☐ _____
☐ _____
☐ _____
☐ _____
☐ _____

17
MONDAY

☐
☐
☐
☐
☐
☐
☐
☐

18
TUESDAY

☐
☐
☐
☐
☐
☐
☐
☐

19
WEDNESDAY

☐
☐
☐
☐
☐
☐
☐
☐

20
THURSDAY

☐
☐
☐
☐
☐
☐
☐
☐

Persistance guarantees that results are inevitable.
– Yogananda

FEBRUARY

21
FRIDAY

- ☐ _____
- ☐ _____
- ☐ _____
- ☐ _____
- ☐ _____
- ☐ _____
- ☐ _____
- ☐ _____

22
SATURDAY

- ☐ _____
- ☐ _____
- ☐ _____
- ☐ _____
- ☐ _____
- ☐ _____
- ☐ _____
- ☐ _____

23
SUNDAY

- ☐ _____
- ☐ _____
- ☐ _____
- ☐ _____
- ☐ _____
- ☐ _____
- ☐ _____
- ☐ _____

MARCH

SUNDAY	MONDAY	TUESDAY	WEDNESDAY
1	2	3	4
8	9	10	11
15	16	17	18
22	23	24	25
29	30	31	

2020

THURSDAY	FRIDAY	SATURDAY	NOTES
5	6	7	☐ _____
			☐ _____
			☐ _____
			☐ _____
			☐ _____
			☐ _____
12	13	14	☐ _____
			☐ _____
			☐ _____
			☐ _____
			☐ _____
			☐ _____
19	20	21	☐ _____
			☐ _____
			☐ _____
			☐ _____
			☐ _____
			☐ _____
26	27	28	

FEBRUARY

S	M	T	W	T	F	S
						1
2	3	4	5	6	7	8
9	10	11	12	13	14	15
16	17	18	19	20	21	22
23	24	25	26	27	28	29

MARCH

S	M	T	W	T	F	S
1	2	3	4	5	6	7
8	9	10	11	12	13	14
15	16	17	18	19	20	21
22	23	24	25	26	27	28
29	30	31				

24
MONDAY

25
TUESDAY

26
WEDNESDAY

27
THURSDAY

I am not afraid, I was born to do this.
– Joan of Arc

28
FRIDAY

- [ ] _____
- [ ] _____
- [ ] _____
- [ ] _____
- [ ] _____
- [ ] _____
- [ ] _____
- [ ] _____

29
SATURDAY

- [ ] _____
- [ ] _____
- [ ] _____
- [ ] _____
- [ ] _____
- [ ] _____
- [ ] _____
- [ ] _____

1
SUNDAY

- [ ] _____
- [ ] _____
- [ ] _____
- [ ] _____
- [ ] _____
- [ ] _____
- [ ] _____
- [ ] _____

2
MONDAY

- [ ]
- [ ]
- [ ]
- [ ]
- [ ]
- [ ]
- [ ]
- [ ]

3
TUESDAY

- [ ]
- [ ]
- [ ]
- [ ]
- [ ]
- [ ]
- [ ]
- [ ]

4
WEDNESDAY

- [ ]
- [ ]
- [ ]
- [ ]
- [ ]
- [ ]
- [ ]
- [ ]

5
THURSDAY

- [ ]
- [ ]
- [ ]
- [ ]
- [ ]
- [ ]
- [ ]
- [ ]

But all of the magic I have known I've had to make myself.

– Shel Silverstein

MARCH

6
FRIDAY

- [ ]
- [ ]
- [ ]
- [ ]
- [ ]
- [ ]
- [ ]
- [ ]

7
SATURDAY

- [ ]
- [ ]
- [ ]
- [ ]
- [ ]
- [ ]
- [ ]
- [ ]

8
SUNDAY

- [ ]
- [ ]
- [ ]
- [ ]
- [ ]
- [ ]
- [ ]
- [ ]

9
MONDAY

☐
☐
☐
☐
☐
☐
☐
☐

10
TUESDAY

☐
☐
☐
☐
☐
☐
☐
☐

11
WEDNESDAY

☐
☐
☐
☐
☐
☐
☐
☐

12
THURSDAY

☐
☐
☐
☐
☐
☐
☐
☐

Somewhere, something incredible is waiting to
be known.
                                    – Carl Sagan

MARCH

13
FRIDAY

- [ ] _____
- [ ] _____
- [ ] _____
- [ ] _____
- [ ] _____
- [ ] _____
- [ ] _____
- [ ] _____

14
SATURDAY

- [ ] _____
- [ ] _____
- [ ] _____
- [ ] _____
- [ ] _____
- [ ] _____
- [ ] _____
- [ ] _____

15
SUNDAY

- [ ] _____
- [ ] _____
- [ ] _____
- [ ] _____
- [ ] _____
- [ ] _____
- [ ] _____
- [ ] _____

16
MONDAY

☐
☐
☐
☐
☐
☐
☐
☐

17
TUESDAY

☐
☐
☐
☐
☐
☐
☐
☐

18
WEDNESDAY

☐
☐
☐
☐
☐
☐
☐
☐

19
THURSDAY

☐
☐
☐
☐
☐
☐
☐
☐

If you can dream it, you can achieve it.
– Zig Ziglar

MARCH

20
FRIDAY

- ☐ _____
- ☐ _____
- ☐ _____
- ☐ _____
- ☐ _____
- ☐ _____
- ☐ _____
- ☐ _____

21
SATURDAY

- ☐ _____
- ☐ _____
- ☐ _____
- ☐ _____
- ☐ _____
- ☐ _____
- ☐ _____
- ☐ _____

22
SUNDAY

- ☐ _____
- ☐ _____
- ☐ _____
- ☐ _____
- ☐ _____
- ☐ _____
- ☐ _____
- ☐ _____

23
MONDAY

- [ ]
- [ ]
- [ ]
- [ ]
- [ ]
- [ ]
- [ ]
- [ ]

24
TUESDAY

- [ ]
- [ ]
- [ ]
- [ ]
- [ ]
- [ ]
- [ ]
- [ ]

25
WEDNESDAY

- [ ]
- [ ]
- [ ]
- [ ]
- [ ]
- [ ]
- [ ]
- [ ]

26
THURSDAY

- [ ]
- [ ]
- [ ]
- [ ]
- [ ]
- [ ]
- [ ]
- [ ]

MARCH

27
FRIDAY

- ☐ _____
- ☐ _____
- ☐ _____
- ☐ _____
- ☐ _____
- ☐ _____
- ☐ _____
- ☐ _____

28
SATURDAY

- ☐ _____
- ☐ _____
- ☐ _____
- ☐ _____
- ☐ _____
- ☐ _____
- ☐ _____
- ☐ _____

29
SUNDAY

- ☐ _____
- ☐ _____
- ☐ _____
- ☐ _____
- ☐ _____
- ☐ _____
- ☐ _____
- ☐ _____

APRIL

SUNDAY	MONDAY	TUESDAY	WEDNESDAY
			1
5	6	7	8
12	13	14	15
19	20	21	22
26	27	28	29

2020

THURSDAY	FRIDAY	SATURDAY	NOTES

THURSDAY   **FRIDAY**   **SATURDAY**   **NOTES**

2   3   4

☐ _____
☐ _____
☐ _____
☐ _____
☐ _____
☐ _____

9   10   11

☐ _____
☐ _____
☐ _____
☐ _____
☐ _____
☐ _____

16   17   18

☐ _____
☐ _____
☐ _____
☐ _____
☐ _____
☐ _____

23   24   25

MARCH

S	M	T	W	T	F	S
1	2	3	4	5	6	7
8	9	10	11	12	13	14
15	16	17	18	19	20	21
22	23	24	25	26	27	28
29	30	31				

30

APRIL

S	M	T	W	T	F	S
			1	2	3	4
5	6	7	8	9	10	11
12	13	14	15	16	17	18
19	20	21	22	23	24	25
26	27	28	29	30		

30
MONDAY

☐
☐
☐
☐
☐
☐
☐
☐

31
TUESDAY

☐
☐
☐
☐
☐
☐
☐
☐

1
WEDNESDAY

☐
☐
☐
☐
☐
☐
☐
☐

2
THURSDAY

☐
☐
☐
☐
☐
☐
☐
☐

Fall seven times and stand up eight.
- Japanese Proverb

MAR-APR

3
FRIDAY

- [ ] _____
- [ ] _____
- [ ] _____
- [ ] _____
- [ ] _____
- [ ] _____
- [ ] _____
- [ ] _____

4
SATURDAY

- [ ] _____
- [ ] _____
- [ ] _____
- [ ] _____
- [ ] _____
- [ ] _____
- [ ] _____
- [ ] _____

5
SUNDAY

- [ ] _____
- [ ] _____
- [ ] _____
- [ ] _____
- [ ] _____
- [ ] _____
- [ ] _____
- [ ] _____

6
MONADY

- [ ]
- [ ]
- [ ]
- [ ]
- [ ]
- [ ]
- [ ]
- [ ]

7
TUESDAY

- [ ]
- [ ]
- [ ]
- [ ]
- [ ]
- [ ]
- [ ]
- [ ]

8
WEDNESDAY

- [ ]
- [ ]
- [ ]
- [ ]
- [ ]
- [ ]
- [ ]
- [ ]

9
THURSDAY

- [ ]
- [ ]
- [ ]
- [ ]
- [ ]
- [ ]
- [ ]
- [ ]

Either you run the day, or the day runs you.
— John Rohn

10 FRIDAY

- ☐ _____
- ☐ _____
- ☐ _____
- ☐ _____
- ☐ _____
- ☐ _____
- ☐ _____
- ☐ _____

11 SATURDAY

- ☐ _____
- ☐ _____
- ☐ _____
- ☐ _____
- ☐ _____
- ☐ _____
- ☐ _____
- ☐ _____

12 SUNDAY

- ☐ _____
- ☐ _____
- ☐ _____
- ☐ _____
- ☐ _____
- ☐ _____
- ☐ _____
- ☐ _____

13
MONDAY

☐
☐
☐
☐
☐
☐
☐
☐

14
TUESDAY

☐
☐
☐
☐
☐
☐
☐
☐

15
WEDNESDAY

☐
☐
☐
☐
☐
☐
☐
☐

16
THURSDAY

☐
☐
☐
☐
☐
☐
☐
☐

When you lose, don't lose the lesson.
– Dalai Lama

17
FRIDAY

- [ ] _____
- [ ] _____
- [ ] _____
- [ ] _____
- [ ] _____
- [ ] _____
- [ ] _____
- [ ] _____

18
SATURDAY

- [ ] _____
- [ ] _____
- [ ] _____
- [ ] _____
- [ ] _____
- [ ] _____
- [ ] _____
- [ ] _____

19
SUNDAY

- [ ] _____
- [ ] _____
- [ ] _____
- [ ] _____
- [ ] _____
- [ ] _____
- [ ] _____
- [ ] _____

20
MONDAY

□
□
□
□
□
□
□
□
□

21
TUESDAY

□
□
□
□
□
□
□
□

22
WEDNESDAY

□
□
□
□
□
□
□
□

23
THURSDAY

□
□
□
□
□
□
□
□

APRIL

24 FRIDAY

- [ ] _____
- [ ] _____
- [ ] _____
- [ ] _____
- [ ] _____
- [ ] _____
- [ ] _____
- [ ] _____

25 SATURDAY

- [ ] _____
- [ ] _____
- [ ] _____
- [ ] _____
- [ ] _____
- [ ] _____
- [ ] _____
- [ ] _____

26 SUNDAY

- [ ] _____
- [ ] _____
- [ ] _____
- [ ] _____
- [ ] _____
- [ ] _____
- [ ] _____
- [ ] _____

MAY

SUNDAY	MONDAY	TUESDAY	WEDNESDAY
3	4	5	6
10	11	12	13
17	18	19	20
24	25	26	27
31			

2020

THURSDAY	FRIDAY	SATURDAY	NOTES
	1	2	☐ _____
			☐ _____
			☐ _____
			☐ _____
			☐ _____
7	8	9	☐ _____
			☐ _____
			☐ _____
			☐ _____
			☐ _____
14	15	16	☐ _____
			☐ _____
			☐ _____
			☐ _____
			☐ _____
21	22	23	☐ _____
			☐ _____
			☐ _____
			☐ _____
			☐ _____
28	29	30	

APRIL

S	M	T	W	T	F	S
			1	2	3	4
5	6	7	8	9	10	11
12	13	14	15	16	17	18
19	20	21	22	23	24	25
26	27	28	29	30		

MAY

S	M	T	W	T	F	S
					1	2
3	4	5	6	7	8	9
10	11	12	13	14	15	16
17	18	19	20	21	22	23
24	25	26	27	28	29	30
31						

27
MONDAY

- ☐
- ☐
- ☐
- ☐
- ☐
- ☐
- ☐
- ☐

28
TUESDAY

- ☐
- ☐
- ☐
- ☐
- ☐
- ☐
- ☐
- ☐

29
WEDNESDAY

- ☐
- ☐
- ☐
- ☐
- ☐
- ☐
- ☐
- ☐

30
THURSDAY

- ☐
- ☐
- ☐
- ☐
- ☐
- ☐
- ☐
- ☐

APR-MAY

1
FRIDAY

- ☐ _____
- ☐ _____
- ☐ _____
- ☐ _____
- ☐ _____
- ☐ _____
- ☐ _____
- ☐ _____

2
SATURDAY

- ☐ _____
- ☐ _____
- ☐ _____
- ☐ _____
- ☐ _____
- ☐ _____
- ☐ _____
- ☐ _____

3
SUNDAY

- ☐ _____
- ☐ _____
- ☐ _____
- ☐ _____
- ☐ _____
- ☐ _____
- ☐ _____
- ☐ _____

4
MONDAY

☐
☐
☐
☐
☐
☐
☐
☐

5
TUESDAY

☐
☐
☐
☐
☐
☐
☐
☐

6
WEDNESDAY

☐
☐
☐
☐
☐
☐
☐
☐

7
THURSDAY

☐
☐
☐
☐
☐
☐
☐
☐

I'm a great believer in luck and I find the harder I
work, the more I have of it.
                              – Thomas Jefferson

MAY

8
FRIDAY

- [ ] _____
- [ ] _____
- [ ] _____
- [ ] _____
- [ ] _____
- [ ] _____
- [ ] _____
- [ ] _____

9
SATURDAY

- [ ] _____
- [ ] _____
- [ ] _____
- [ ] _____
- [ ] _____
- [ ] _____
- [ ] _____
- [ ] _____

10
SUNDAY

- [ ] _____
- [ ] _____
- [ ] _____
- [ ] _____
- [ ] _____
- [ ] _____
- [ ] _____
- [ ] _____

11
MONDAY

☐
☐
☐
☐
☐
☐
☐
☐

12
TUESDAY

☐
☐
☐
☐
☐
☐
☐
☐

13
WEDNESDAY

☐
☐
☐
☐
☐
☐
☐
☐

14
THURSDAY

☐
☐
☐
☐
☐
☐
☐
☐

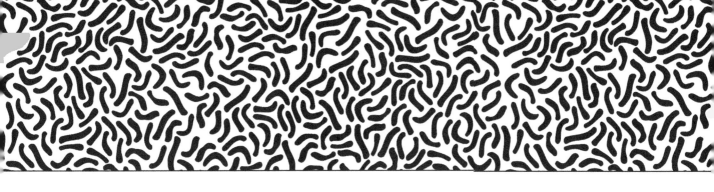

Dreaming, after all, is a form of planning.
— Gloria Steinem

MAY

15
FRIDAY

☐ _____
☐ _____
☐ _____
☐ _____
☐ _____
☐ _____
☐ _____
☐ _____

16
SATURDAY

☐ _____
☐ _____
☐ _____
☐ _____
☐ _____
☐ _____
☐ _____
☐ _____

17
SUNDAY

☐ _____
☐ _____
☐ _____
☐ _____
☐ _____
☐ _____
☐ _____
☐ _____

18
MONDAY

19
TUESDAY

20
WEDNESDAY

21
THURSDAY

- ☐
- ☐
- ☐
- ☐
- ☐
- ☐
- ☐
- ☐

- ☐
- ☐
- ☐
- ☐
- ☐
- ☐
- ☐
- ☐

- ☐
- ☐
- ☐
- ☐
- ☐
- ☐
- ☐
- ☐

- ☐
- ☐
- ☐
- ☐
- ☐
- ☐
- ☐
- ☐

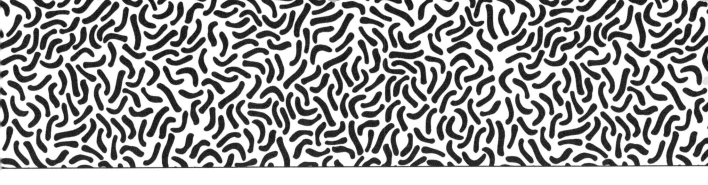

There are no traffic jams along the extra mile.
— Roger Staubach

MAY

22
FRIDAY

☐ _____
☐ _____
☐ _____
☐ _____
☐ _____
☐ _____
☐ _____
☐ _____

23
SATURDAY

☐ _____
☐ _____
☐ _____
☐ _____
☐ _____
☐ _____
☐ _____
☐ _____

24
SUNDAY

☐ _____
☐ _____
☐ _____
☐ _____
☐ _____
☐ _____
☐ _____
☐ _____

25
MONDAY

☐
☐
☐
☐
☐
☐
☐
☐

26
TUESDAY

☐
☐
☐
☐
☐
☐
☐
☐

27
WEDNESDAY

☐
☐
☐
☐
☐
☐
☐
☐

28
THURSDAY

☐
☐
☐
☐
☐
☐
☐
☐

Your time is limited, so don't waste it living someone else's life.

– Steve Jobs

MAY

29
FRIDAY

- [ ] _____
- [ ] _____
- [ ] _____
- [ ] _____
- [ ] _____
- [ ] _____
- [ ] _____
- [ ] _____

30
SATURDAY

- [ ] _____
- [ ] _____
- [ ] _____
- [ ] _____
- [ ] _____
- [ ] _____
- [ ] _____
- [ ] _____

31
SUNDAY

- [ ] _____
- [ ] _____
- [ ] _____
- [ ] _____
- [ ] _____
- [ ] _____
- [ ] _____
- [ ] _____

JUNE

SUNDAY	MONDAY	TUESDAY	WEDNESDAY
	1	2	3
7	8	9	10
14	15	16	17
21	22	23	24
28	29	30	

2020

THURSDAY	FRIDAY	SATURDAY	NOTES
4	5	6	☐ _____
			☐ _____
			☐ _____
			☐ _____
			☐ _____
			☐ _____
11	12	13	☐ _____
			☐ _____
			☐ _____
			☐ _____
			☐ _____
			☐ _____
18	19	20	☐ _____
			☐ _____
			☐ _____
			☐ _____
			☐ _____
25	26	27	☐ _____

MAY

S	M	T	W	T	F	S
					1	2
3	4	5	6	7	8	9
10	11	12	13	14	15	16
17	18	19	20	21	22	23
24	25	26	27	28	29	30
31						

JUNE

S	M	T	W	T	F	S
	1	2	3	4	5	6
7	8	9	10	11	12	13
14	15	16	17	18	19	20
21	22	23	24	25	26	27
28	29	30				

1
MONODY

☐
☐
☐
☐
☐
☐
☐
☐

2
TUESDAY

☐
☐
☐
☐
☐
☐
☐
☐

3
WEDNESDAY

☐
☐
☐
☐
☐
☐
☐
☐

4
THURSDAY

☐
☐
☐
☐
☐
☐
☐
☐

Every strike brings me closer to the next home run.

                – Babe Ruth

JUNE

5
FRIDAY

- ☐
- ☐
- ☐
- ☐
- ☐
- ☐
- ☐
- ☐

6
SATURDAY

- ☐
- ☐
- ☐
- ☐
- ☐
- ☐
- ☐
- ☐

7
SUNDAY

- ☐
- ☐
- ☐
- ☐
- ☐
- ☐
- ☐
- ☐

8
MONADAY

☐
☐
☐
☐
☐
☐
☐
☐

9
TUESDAY

☐
☐
☐
☐
☐
☐
☐
☐

10
WEDNESDAY

☐
☐
☐
☐
☐
☐
☐
☐

11
THURSDAY

☐
☐
☐
☐
☐
☐
☐
☐

Yesterday is not ours to recover, but tomorrow is
ours to win or lose.

– Lyndon B. Johnson

JUNE

12
FRIDAY

- [ ] _____
- [ ] _____
- [ ] _____
- [ ] _____
- [ ] _____
- [ ] _____
- [ ] _____
- [ ] _____

13
SATURDAY

- [ ] _____
- [ ] _____
- [ ] _____
- [ ] _____
- [ ] _____
- [ ] _____
- [ ] _____
- [ ] _____

14
SUNDAY

- [ ] _____
- [ ] _____
- [ ] _____
- [ ] _____
- [ ] _____
- [ ] _____
- [ ] _____
- [ ] _____

15
MONADY

_____

_____
_____
_____
_____
_____
_____

☐ _____
☐ _____
☐ _____
☐ _____
☐ _____
☐ _____
☐ _____
☐ _____

16
TUESDAY

_____
_____
_____
_____
_____
_____
_____
_____

☐ _____
☐ _____
☐ _____
☐ _____
☐ _____
☐ _____
☐ _____
☐ _____

17
WEDNESDAY

_____
_____
_____
_____
_____
_____
_____
_____

☐ _____
☐ _____
☐ _____
☐ _____
☐ _____
☐ _____
☐ _____
☐ _____

18
THURSDAY

_____
_____
_____
_____
_____
_____
_____
_____

☐ _____
☐ _____
☐ _____
☐ _____
☐ _____
☐ _____
☐ _____
☐ _____

Be happy for this moment. This moment is your life.

– Omar Khayyam

JUNE

19
FRIDAY

20
SATURDAY

21
SUNDAY

22
MONODAY

- [ ]
- [ ]
- [ ]
- [ ]
- [ ]
- [ ]
- [ ]
- [ ]

23
TUESDAY

- [ ]
- [ ]
- [ ]
- [ ]
- [ ]
- [ ]
- [ ]
- [ ]

24
WEDNESDAY

- [ ]
- [ ]
- [ ]
- [ ]
- [ ]
- [ ]
- [ ]
- [ ]

25
THURSDAY

- [ ]
- [ ]
- [ ]
- [ ]
- [ ]
- [ ]
- [ ]
- [ ]

Every day brings new choices.

– Martha Beck

JUNE

26
FRIDAY

- [ ] _____
- [ ] _____
- [ ] _____
- [ ] _____
- [ ] _____
- [ ] _____
- [ ] _____
- [ ] _____

27
SATURDAY

- [ ] _____
- [ ] _____
- [ ] _____
- [ ] _____
- [ ] _____
- [ ] _____
- [ ] _____
- [ ] _____

28
SUNDAY

- [ ] _____
- [ ] _____
- [ ] _____
- [ ] _____
- [ ] _____
- [ ] _____
- [ ] _____
- [ ] _____

29
MONDAY

30
TUESDAY

1
WEDNESDAY

2
THURSDAY

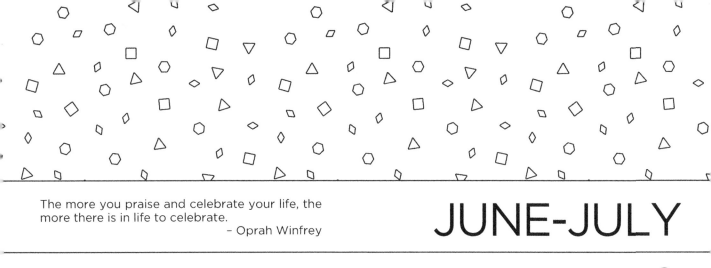

The more you praise and celebrate your life, the
more there is in life to celebrate.
— Oprah Winfrey

JUNE-JULY

3
FRIDAY

☐
☐
☐
☐
☐
☐
☐
☐

4
SATURDAY

☐
☐
☐
☐
☐
☐
☐
☐

5
SUNDAY

☐
☐
☐
☐
☐
☐
☐
☐

Made in the USA
Columbia, SC
05 February 2021